Turkey

A Fun and Educational Book for Kids with Amazing Facts and Pictures

Table of Contents

Introduction

Large domesticated birds are native to North America, including the turkey bird. It is a member of the genus Meleagris and has a strong kinship with other game birds including pheasants, quails, and grouse. The largest game bird in North America, the wild turkey can be found all over the United States, Mexico, and Canada.

The turkey bird is renowned for its unusual looks, which include a featherless head and neck that are embellished with vivid red and blue skin. The magnificent display of feathers and colors that male turkeys, commonly referred to as toms, put on during breeding season is what attracts females. Hens, or female turkeys, are smaller and usually have fewer colorful feathers.

A typical food source, turkeys are frequently eaten on special occasions like Thanksgiving and Christmas. In addition, they are raised for their pets, feathers, and eggs. Given its high protein content and low fat content, turkey meat is a popular healthy option.

Scientific Name

The turkey bird's scientific name is Meleagris gallopavo.

Appearance

The turkey bird, especially the male bird or tom, has a distinctive appearance. The turkey has the following distinguishing physical characteristics:

Size: A mature male turkey's wingspan can reach 5 feet and he can weigh up to 25 pounds. Smaller and weighing up to 12 pounds, females are called hens.

The color of the turkey's feathers might vary, but most of them have black, iridescent feathers with a metallic shine. Feathers on male turkeys are more vivid and vibrant than those on female turkeys, which are more muted in hue.

The turkey's head and neck lack feathers and have skin that is a vibrant red, blue, and white color. To entice ladies, male turkeys can expand or contract their snood, a fleshy protrusion on their head.

Beak: The long, pointed beak of the turkey is used for probing and pecking for food.

Legs and Feet: The turkey's long, strong legs are employed for short-distance sprinting, walking, and flying. Sharp claws on the foot are utilized for perching and scraping.

The turkey is an impressive-looking bird overall, particularly during the breeding season when the male turkey exhibits his vibrant skin and feathers to draw females.

Geography

Native to North America, the wild turkey's natural habitat stretches from southern Canada to northern Mexico. The majority of the eastern United States, as well as portions of the west and Mexico, are included in the turkey's range. It is possible to find turkeys in a number of settings, such as forests, grasslands, and agricultural areas. Turkeys are adaptable birds.

Due to habitat degradation and killing, the wild turkey was once on the verge of extinction, but conservation initiatives have helped to increase their population. The United States currently has wild turkeys in each of its 50 states, and they are frequently grown for meat on farms.

Moreover, turkeys have been brought to other continents, such as Europe, where they are farmed for their meat. They have also been imported as a game bird to other regions of the world, like as New Zealand, where they are hunted for fun.

Behavior

Turkeys are intelligent and gregarious birds that display a variety of fascinating behaviors. The following are some of the distinctive turkey behaviors:

Roosting: To evade predators, turkeys spend the night in trees. At dusk, they will soar into the treetops, and at dawn, they will descend.

Turkeys are sociable creatures that flock together; these flocks can contain anywhere from a few to hundreds of turkeys. A dominant male or tom and one or more hens make up most flocks.

Male turkeys strut to attract females during the breeding season. They move in a circular manner, puffing out their feathers, fanning out their tails, and gobbling.

Dust bathing: To keep their feathers clean and parasite-free, turkeys take dust baths. They roll around in the sand while making a hole in the earth.

Turkeys can fly despite their size, and they typically do so to avoid danger or roost in trees.

Turkeys are loud birds that produce a range of noises, such as yelping, gobbling, and purring. They communicate with one another and establish supremacy via these noises.

All things considered, turkeys are intriguing birds with intricate social structures and special adaptations that enable them to live in a range of habitats.

Reproduction

The mating system of turkeys is distinctive, and they display unusual reproductive habits. Their reproductive biology is notable for the following reasons:

Breeding Season: Male turkeys will strut and flaunt their feathers to entice ladies during the breeding season, which normally occurs in the spring.

Male turkeys will blow out their feathers, fan their tails, and drag their wings during courting, all the while gobbling. To display their plumage, they would also spin around the female while dancing.

Nesting: After a male turkey, or tom, has courted a female turkey, or hen, she will construct a ground nest in a remote location, like a brush pile or tall grass.

Laying a clutch: The female turkey lays a clutch of 8–15 eggs, which she then incubates for about 28 days until they hatch. The hen will only leave the nest to eat once per day while the egg is being incubated.

Parental Care: A day or two after the eggs hatch, the young turkeys, or poults, are ready to leave the nest. The hen will take care of and guard the young until they are strong enough to survive on their own, which often takes many weeks.

Male turkeys have a polygynous mating system, which means that during the breeding season, they will mate with various females. More females will be attracted to and mated with by dominant males than subordinate males.

Overall, the fascinating and intricate reproductive biology of turkeys includes distinctive mating behaviors, nesting practices, and parental care techniques.

Social Life

Due to their sociable nature, turkeys display a range of amusing social behaviors. The following standout features of their social life:

Turkeys live in flocks that can number anything from a few to hundreds of birds. One or more dominant males, known as toms, and numerous females, known as hens, often make up flocks.

There is a hierarchy among the birds in a flock, with the dominant birds at the top and the inferior birds at the bottom. Dominant men will establish their position by acting aggressively and engaging in courtship rituals.

Communication: Gobbles, clucks, and purrs are just a few of the vocalizations turkeys use to talk to one another. Also, they communicate their intentions through their body language, such as puffing out their feathers or fanning out their tails.

To avoid predators, turkeys often roost in groups on trees at night. In order to establish their authority throughout the flock, the dominant males frequently roost in higher branches.

Dust bathing is a common practice among turkeys and is a crucial social behavior that keeps the birds' feathers healthy and free of parasites.

Fights: To establish their dominance among the flock, dominant males will occasionally engage in combat with one another. These altercations can be deadly and leave victims with injuries or even death.

Turkeys are often social birds that display a range of fascinating social behaviors. Their hierarchy, flocking, and communication shed light on their intricate social structures.

Habitat

The adaptive birds known as turkeys live in a wide range of settings, from forests and grasslands to agricultural areas and suburban communities. The following are some of the main environments where you can find turkeys:

Forests: Turkeys frequently inhabit mature woods with open understory vegetation that offers cover and potential nesting locations. Although they are more common in deciduous and pine woods, they can also be found in mixed hardwood and coniferous forests.

Grasslands: Prairies and meadows are examples of grassland ecosystems where turkeys can also be found. These environments offer areas that are accessible for breeding and foraging.

Turkeys are frequently seen in agricultural settings, like fields and pastures, where they can graze on crops and insects. They are frequently reared in farms to provide meat.

Turkeys are versatile creatures that can also be found in suburban and urban environments, where they may eat seeds, insects, and decorative plants.

Nevertheless, as long as the environments offer enough cover, food, and nesting places, turkeys are able to adapt to a variety of varied settings. Yet, depending on the season, climate, and resource availability, they may have different habitat preferences.

Senses

Turkeys have highly developed senses that enable them to move through their surroundings and identify potential dangers. The following are some noteworthy features of their sensory capacities:

With their eyes set on the sides of their heads, turkeys have superb eyesight and a broad field of vision. They are able to recognize food and potential mates thanks to their ability to sense movement at a distance and their full-color vision.

Hearing: Turkeys have keen hearing and are able to distinguish distant sounds. They can detect the vocalizations of predators and employ a variety of vocalizations to communicate with one another.

Smell: Compared to many other animals, turkeys have a subpar sense of smell. They are still able to pick up some scents, particularly those connected to food and predators.

Touch: Turkeys' sense of touch is highly developed,

especially on their head and beak. They pick up objects and use their beak to pick them up and move them around their habitat.

Generally, to traverse their habitat and identify potential hazards, turkeys mostly rely on their vision and hearing. Although having a limited sense of smell, they have a highly developed sense of touch that allows them to interact with their surroundings.

Feeding

Since turkeys are omnivores, they consume both plant- and animal-based diets. Following are some noteworthy characteristics of their eating behaviors:

A variety of foods, including seeds, nuts, berries, fruits, insects, small mammals, and reptiles, are consumed by turkeys. Moreover, they will consume small amphibians like salamanders and frogs.

Turkeys spend a lot of time on the ground foraging for food, using their acute vision to find prospective food items. To find food buried in the earth, they would also scratch the ground with their foot.

Seasonal Variation: Depending on the time of year and the food supply, turkey diets might change. For instance, they might predominately consume plants and insects in the spring and summer while switching to a diet heavier in seeds and nuts in the fall and winter.

Eating Habits: Turkeys frequently eat in groups, which can number anything from a few to hundreds of birds. As a means of feeding on the plants and insects that are disturbed by the activities of other animals, such deer, they will occasionally follow them.

Domesticated Turkeys: A diet rich in grains and other animal feed is frequently given to domesticated turkeys. To make sure they get all the essential nutrients, they are occasionally also given supplements.

All things considered, turkeys are flexible feeders who will consume a range of plant- and animal-based diets based on the season and the availability of food. As expert foragers, they will use their strong senses to find prospective food sources on the ground.

Diet

As omnivores, turkeys eat both plant- and animal-based foods in their diversified diet. Some of the essential elements in their diet are as follows:

Acorns, beechnuts, and hickory nuts are just a few of the seeds and nuts that turkeys eat. Mast crops, which are the fruits and nuts that trees produce, are particularly beloved by them.

Fruits and berries: Grapes, blueberries, and strawberries are just a few of the fruits and berries that turkeys eat. To find these foods, they frequently forage in open spaces like fields and meadows.

Turkeys will consume a wide range of insects and other invertebrates, such as grasshoppers, crickets, ants, and beetles. Snails, slugs, and other small invertebrates will also be eaten by them.

Small Mammals and Reptiles: Turkeys are opportunistic

feeders and will occasionally consume both tiny reptiles like snakes and lizards as well as small mammals like mice and voles.

Domesticated Turkeys: A diet rich in grains and other animal feed is frequently given to domesticated turkeys. To make sure they get all the required nutrients, they could also be given supplements.

Generally, turkeys can live in a variety of various ecosystems thanks to their wide and adaptive diet. As expert foragers, they will use their strong senses to find prospective food sources on the ground.

Babies

Poults, or baby turkeys, are produced from the eggs laid by female turkeys. These are some important details regarding turkey babies:

The incubation period for turkey eggs is about 28 days. The female turkey incubates the eggs during this period, keeping them warm and rotating them frequently to make sure the developing embryos receive enough oxygen and nourishment.

Hatching: After a few hours of one another, the poults break through the eggshell when the eggs hatch. They have delicate, downy feathers covering them, and they can move around and vocalize nearly right away.

Care: The mother turkey tends to her young, keeping them warm and guiding them to sources of food and water. Although he spends less time caring for the poults, the male turkey may still offer some protection.

Growth: Within a few weeks of hatching, young birds can fly

short distances thanks to their rapid growth. They normally spend several months with their mother, gradually changing their nutrition to resemble that of adult turkeys.

Domesticated Turkeys: To make sure domesticated turkey poults get all the nutrients they need, they are frequently grown in incubators and may be given a specific diet. Until they are completely mature, they are usually kept apart from adult turkeys.

Yet, during their first few weeks of life, turkey chicks still need on their mother for care and safety. Generally, turkey infants are highly independent from birth. They progressively switch to a diet that is more like that of adult turkeys as they get bigger, more independent creatures.

Predators

There are a number of natural predators that turkeys may encounter throughout their lifetimes. Here are a few typical turkey predators:

Coyotes: One of the most frequent predators of turkeys, coyotes will feed on young and old birds alike.

Foxes: Young turkeys are particularly vulnerable to fox predation.

Raccoons: Raccoons are opportunistic hunters that prey on turkeys, especially young ones.

Bobcats: Skilled hunters, bobcats occasionally prey on turkeys.

Hawks and owls: During the winter months, when food is scarce, raptors like hawks and owls prey on mature turkeys.

Domesticated Dogs: In rural regions where they are let to roam freely, domesticated dogs can be a hazard to turkeys.

In general, a range of predators, both on the ground and in the air, feed on turkeys. They have developed a variety of adaptations, like as their short-range flight abilities and their acute vision and hearing senses, to assist them avoid or flee from predators. Predation, however, still poses a serious threat to wild turkey populations.

Evolution

It is thought that turkeys first appeared in North America more than 11 million years ago. They are believed to have originated from the Galliformes order of ground-dwelling birds, which also includes chickens, quails, and pheasants.

According to fossil evidence, early turkey progenitors were smaller and had longer legs than contemporary turkeys do now. Larger and more robust turkeys have evolved over time, most likely as a result of changes in their habitat and food.

A variety of adaptations have also evolved in turkeys to help them thrive in their environment. For instance, their great hearing and vision aid them in spotting potential predators, and their ability to fly short distances enables them to flee from harm.

The evolution of turkeys has been significantly influenced by humans over time. Because domesticated turkeys have been intentionally developed for particular characteristics, such as larger size and quicker growth rates, they stand out from their wild counterparts.

Overall, there are many ecological, environmental, and human factors that have influenced the evolution of turkeys throughout time. Despite having a lengthy history, turkeys have continued to change and adapt to their surroundings.

Population

Species and geographic differences have an impact on the turkey population. The wild turkey (Meleagris gallopavo) and the ocellated turkey (Meleagris ocellata) are two kinds of turkey that can be found all over the world.

Much of North America is home to the wild turkey, which is thought to have a population of 7 million birds. Hunting and habitat loss caused a significant decline in the wild turkey population in the early 1900s, but conservation initiatives and reintroduction projects have helped to increase their numbers in many places.

Only the Yucatan Peninsula of Mexico, Belize, and Guatemala are home to the ocellated turkey. 300,000 birds are thought to be living there.

There are domesticated turkeys kept for their flesh, eggs, and feathers all around the world. The number of domesticated turkeys in the world is thought to number in the billions.

Generally, habitat degradation, killing, and other challenges continue to represent a threat to the long-term survival of wild turkeys, despite the fact that their number has recovered in many places. Turkey populations must be kept healthy and their place in ecosystems must be preserved through conservation initiatives and environmentally sound management techniques.

Conservation Status

Depending on the species and area, different turkeys have different conservation statuses. These are some of the most well-known turkey species' conservation statuses:

Wild Turkey (Meleagris gallopavo): The International Union for Conservation of Nature has classified the wild turkey as a species of "least concern" (IUCN). Nonetheless, several subspecies of wild turkey, such as the Florida subspecies (Meleagris gallopavo osceola) and the Mexico subspecies, are regarded as being at risk (Meleagris gallopavo gallopavo).

Ocellated Turkey (Meleagris ocellata): Although the IUCN lists the ocellated turkey as a species of "least concern," it is nevertheless thought to be in danger because of habitat loss and poaching in some locations.

Due to its widespread farming and breeding for human consumption, the domesticated turkey (Meleagris gallopavo domestica) is not categorized as a threatened or endangered species.

Overall, habitat degradation, hunting, and other challenges continue to represent a threat to the long-term survival of the wild turkey and the ocellated turkey, despite the fact that they are not currently thought to be in danger of going extinct. Turkey populations must be kept healthy and their place in ecosystems must be preserved through conservation initiatives and environmentally sound management techniques.

Health

Many health problems can affect turkeys, both in the wild and in captivity. The following are some of the most typical turkey health issues:

Several respiratory illnesses, including avian influenza, mycoplasma, and infectious bronchitis, can affect turkeys.

Turkeys are susceptible to both external and internal parasites, such as mites, lice, and worms.

Nutritional deficiencies: Poor nutrition can cause turkeys to experience reproductive problems, low growth, and feather loss.

Heat stress: Turkeys are susceptible to heat exhaustion, which can cause them to become lethargic, dehydrate, and even die.

Disorders of the feet and legs: Turkeys are prone to foot and leg issues like bumblefoot and twisted legs, which can impair their mobility and general health.

Good management techniques are necessary to prevent health issues in turkeys, including appropriate diet, housing, and sanitation. To stop the spread of diseases and to guarantee the welfare of individual birds as well as flocks, prompt identification and treatment of any health issues are also crucial. A veterinarian should be consulted in order to create a thorough health management plan for your turkeys. Vaccines are available for various diseases that affect turkeys.

Lifespan

Depending on the species and whether they are domesticated or wild, turkeys have different life spans. Following are some estimations of the average lifetime of various turkey species:

Wild Turkey (Meleagris gallopavo): Although some have been known to live longer, wild turkeys can live up to 3–4 years in the wild.

Ocellated Turkey (Meleagris ocellata): Ocellated turkeys live about three to four years on average, which is comparable to wild turkeys.

Melagris gallopavo domestica, sometimes known as the domesticated turkey, is a bird that has been developed specifically for its ability to produce meat. Its lifespan is shorter than that of the wild turkey. Although some can live longer in perfect circumstances, they normally only have a lifespan of two to three years.

The longevity of turkeys can be impacted by a variety of

factors, including genetics, nutrition, housing, and the presence of sickness or other health problems. Whether they are domesticated or wild, turkeys can enjoy healthy and productive lives with the right care and management.

Conclusion

To sum up, turkeys are an interesting and varied group of birds with a long history of contact with people. Turkeys have captivated our attention and imagination for ages thanks to their unique appearance and behavior as well as their significant role in ecosystems and agriculture. Several turkey species are threatened by extinction, but others have been successfully tamed and bred for food. Turkeys, whether wild or domesticated, require adequate care and management, just like any other animal, to ensure their health and well-being.